PITCHED BATTLE PROFILES

On the following pages you will find the Pitched Battle profiles for most of the units that can be used in games of Warhammer Age of Sigmar. The rules for using Pitched Battle profiles can be found in section 25.0 of the core rules.

The Pitched Battle profiles are organised first by Grand Alliance and then alphabetically by faction. There are four Grand Alliances: Order, Chaos, Death and Destruction. The Grand Alliance to which a unit belongs is determined by the first keyword listed on the keywords line on its warscroll. For example, the first keyword on the Vindictors warscroll is ORDER, so the Pitched Battle profile for a Vindictors unit can be found in the 'Order' section of this book and, as the unit belongs to the Stormcast Eternals faction, its entry is in the Stormcast Eternals table.

The profiles for endless spells that are not faction-specific appear in the 'Additional Pitched Battle Profiles' section at the end of this booklet.

BATTLEFIELD ROLES

Battlefield roles are important because they often determine which units you can include in your army, depending upon the army selection rules in the battlepack you are using. To make it easier for you to pick which units you wish to include in your army, the entries within each Pitched Battle profiles table are grouped by battlefield role (see section 25.5 of the core rules for more information on battlefield roles).

The different battlefield roles are as follows:

Artillery: These are units that are capable of making powerful, long-range shooting attacks.

Battleline: These units form the core of their faction's armies.

Behemoth: Behemoths are extremely large and powerful units that have a dominating presence upon the battlefield.

Leader: As the name suggests, Leaders are units that can command their fellow warriors in battle.

ALLIES TABLES

Below a faction's Pitched Battle profiles table, you will find a list of allies that can be taken in an army from that faction (core rules, 25.8 and 27.1). If an entry in an allies table is simply a faction name, it means that any unit from that faction can be taken as an allied unit in an army from the faction with which the allies table is associated.

Many allies tables also specify restrictions on which units from a listed faction can be taken as allies. Similarly, if you pick a subfaction for your army, this may prevent you from taking certain units as allies.

When we republish a set of Pitched Battle profiles, the new version takes precedence over versions with an earlier publication date or no publication date.

ORDER

CITES OF SIGMAR				
WARSCROLL	UNIT SIZE	POINTS	BATTLEFIELD ROLE	NOTES
Bleakswords	10	95	Battleline	
Darkshards	10	115	Battleline	
Dreadspears	10	90	Battleline	
Eternal Guard	10	125	Battleline	
Freeguild Crossbowmen	10	105	Battleline	
Freeguild Guard	10	85	Battleline	
Freeguild Handgunners	10	105	Battleline	
Ironbreakers	10	115	Battleline	
Longbeards	10	105	Battleline	
Helblaster Volley Gun	1	125	Artillery	Single
Helstorm Rocket Battery	1	135	Artillery	Single
Celestial Hurricanum	1	230	Behemoth	Single
Flamespyre Phoenix	1	205	Behemoth	Single
Frostheart Phoenix	1	220	Behemoth	Single
Kharibdyss	1	165	Behemoth	Single. Battleline in an Anvilgard army
Luminark of Hysh	1	220	Behemoth	Single
Steam Tank	1	195	Behemoth	Single. Battleline if general is a Steam Tank with Commander
War Hydra	1	170	Behemoth	Single. Battleline in an Anvilgard army
Anointed	1	110	Leader	Single
Assassin	1	80	Leader	Single
Battlemage	1	115	Leader	Single
Black Ark Fleetmaster	1	70	Leader	Single
Cogsmith	1	70	Leader	Single
Doralia ven Denst	1	115	Leader	Single
Freeguild General	1	100	Leader	Single
Galen ven Denst	1	115	Leader	Single
Nomad Prince	1	110	Leader	Single
Runelord	1	100	Leader	Single
Sorceress	1	95	Leader	Single
Warden King	1	100	Leader	Single
Anointed on Flamespyre Phoenix	1	290	Leader, Behemoth	Single
Anointed on Frostheart Phoenix	1	315	Leader, Behemoth	Single
Battlemage on Griffon	1	275	Leader, Behemoth	Single
Celestial Hurricanum with Celestial Battlemage	1	280	Leader, Behemoth	Single
Dreadlord on Black Dragon	1	290	Leader, Behemoth	Single
Freeguild General on Griffon	1	305	Leader, Behemoth	Single
Luminark of Hysh with White Battlemage	1	275	Leader, Behemoth	Single
Sorceress on Black Dragon	1	295	Leader, Behemoth	Single
Steam Tank with Commander	1	230	Leader, Behemoth	Single
Black Ark Corsairs	10	85		Battleline if general is a Black Ark Fleetmaster
Black Guard	10	135		Battleline if general is DARKLING COVENS
Dark Riders	5	115		Battleline if general is SHADOWBLADES
Demigryph Knights	3	175		Battleline if general is FREEGUILD

CITIES OF SIGMAR

WARSCROLL	UNIT SIZE	POINTS	BATTLEFIELD ROLE	NOTES
Drakespawn Chariots	1	80		Battleline if general is ORDER SERPENTIS
Drakespawn Knights	5	125		Battleline if general is ORDER SERPENTIS
Executioners	10	130		Battleline if general is DARKLING COVENS
Flagellants	10	80		Battleline if general is HUMAN
Freeguild Greatswords	10	150		Battleline if general is FREEGUILD
Freeguild Outriders	5	110		Battleline in a Tempest's Eye army
Freeguild Pistoliers	5	105		Battleline in a Tempest's Eye army
Gyrobombers	1	90		
Gyrocopters	1	75		
Hammerers	10	145		Battleline if general is DISPOSSESSED
Irondrakes	10	160		Battleline if general is DUARDIN
Phoenix Guard	10	175		Battleline if general is PHOENIX TEMPLE
Scourgerunner Chariots	1	80		Battleline if general is SCOURGE PRIVATEERS
Shadow Warriors	10	120		Battleline if general is SHADOWBLADES
Sisters of the Thorn	5	130		Battleline if general is WANDERERS
Sisters of the Watch	10	180		Battleline if general is WANDERERS
Wild Riders	5	120		Battleline if general is WANDERERS
Wildwood Rangers	10	135		Battleline if general is WANDERERS

FACTION	ALLIES
Cities of Sigmar	Daughters of Khaine, Fyreslayers, Idoneth Deepkin, Kharadron Overlords (except in Tempest's Eye armies), Sylvaneth (except in Living City and Greywater Fastness armies)

WARSCROLL	UNIT SIZE	POINTS	BATTLEFIELD ROLE	NOTES
Gotrek Gurnisson	1	435		Single, Unique. This unit can be included as an ally in any army that has an ORDER general. If this unit is included in an army, no other allied units can be included in the army. You can include Gotrek Gurnisson in a Pitched Battle army even if his points cost exceeds the amount allowed for allied units.

DAUGHTERS OF KHAINE				
WARSCROLL	UNIT SIZE	POINTS	BATTLEFIELD ROLE	NOTES
Sisters of Slaughter	10	135	Battleline	
Witch Aelves	10	120	Battleline	
Avatar of Khaine	1	135	Behemoth	Single
Bloodwrack Medusa	1	120	Leader	Single
Hag Queen	1	105	Leader	Single
Melusai Ironscale	1	115	Leader	Single
Morathi-Khaine	1	660	Leader	Single, Unique. These units must be taken as a set. Although taken as a set, each is a separate unit.
The Shadow Queen	1		Leader, Behemoth	
Morgwaeth the Bloodied	1	175	Leader	Single, Unique. These units must be taken as a set. Although taken as a set, each is a separate unit.
The Blade Coven	4			
Slaughter Queen	1	120	Leader	Single
Bloodwrack Shrine	1	190	Leader, Behemoth	Single
Hag Queen on Cauldron of Blood	1	255	Leader, Behemoth	Single
Slaughter Queen on Cauldron of Blood	1	300	Leader, Behemoth	Single
Blood Sisters	5	140		Battleline if general is a **BLOODWRACK MEDUSA** or Melusai Ironscale
Blood Stalkers	5	170		Battleline if general is a **BLOODWRACK MEDUSA** or Melusai Ironscale
Doomfire Warlocks	5	140		
Khainite Shadowstalkers	9	120		
Khinerai Heartrenders	5	95		
Khinerai Lifetakers	5	90		
Bladewind	-	80	*Endless Spell*	
Bloodwrack Viper	-	95	*Endless Spell*	
Heart of Fury	-	55	*Invocation*	

FACTION	ALLIES
Daughters of Khaine	Cities of Sigmar, Idoneth Deepkin

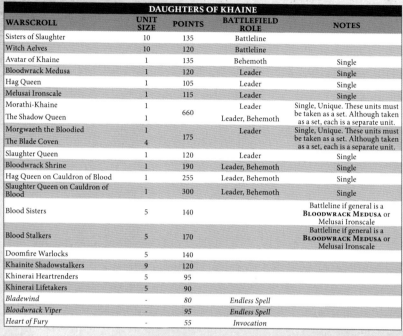

WARSCROLL	UNIT SIZE	POINTS	BATTLEFIELD ROLE	NOTES
FYRESLAYERS				
Vulkite Berzerkers	10	160	Battleline	
Auric Runefather	1	100	Leader	Single
Auric Runemaster	1	115	Leader	Single
Auric Runesmiter	1	120	Leader	Single
Auric Runeson	1	90	Leader	Single
Battlesmith	1	125	Leader	Single
Fjul-Grimnir	1	150	Leader	Single, Unique. These units must be taken as a set. Although taken as a set, each is a separate unit.
The Chosen Axes	3			
Auric Runefather on Magmadroth	1	285	Leader, Behemoth	Single
Auric Runesmiter on Magmadroth	1	275	Leader, Behemoth	Single
Auric Runeson on Magmadroth	1	240	Leader, Behemoth	Single
Auric Hearthguard	5	125		Battleline if general is an Auric Runemaster
Doomseeker	1	95		Single
Grimwrath Berzerker	1	120		Single
Hearthguard Berzerkers	5	125		Battleline if general is **AURIC RUNEFATHER**
Molten Infernoth	-	*75*	*Invocation*	
Runic Fyrewall	-	*60*	*Invocation*	
Zharrgron Flame-spitter	-	*60*	*Invocation*	
Magmic Battleforge	-	*0*	*Faction Terrain Feature*	

FACTION	ALLIES
Fyreslayers	Cities of Sigmar (**DISPOSSESSED** and **IRONWELD ARSENAL** units only), Kharadron Overlords, Stormcast Eternals

7

IDONETH DEEPKIN

WARSCROLL	UNIT SIZE	POINTS	BATTLEFIELD ROLE	NOTES
Namarti Thralls	10	120	Battleline	
Akhelian Leviadon	1	380	Behemoth	Single
Akhelian King	1	230	Leader	Single
Eidolon of Mathlann, Aspect of the Sea	1	355	Leader	Single
Eidolon of Mathlann, Aspect of the Storm	1	330	Leader	Single
Elathain Ill-fated	1	145	Leader	Single, Unique. These units must be taken as a set. Although taken as a set, each is a separate unit.
Elathain's Soulraid	3			
Isharann Soulrender	1	90	Leader	Single
Isharann Soulscryer	1	140	Leader	Single
Isharann Tidecaster	1	105	Leader	Single
Lotann, Warden of the Soul Ledgers	1	75	Leader	Single, Unique
Volturnos, High King of the Deep	1	260	Leader	Single, Unique
Akhelian Allopexes	1	125		
Akhelian Ishlaen Guard	3	155		Battleline if general is an **AKHELIAN HERO**
Akhelian Morrsarr Guard	3	195		Battleline if general is an **AKHELIAN HERO**
Namarti Reavers	10	115		Battleline if general is an **ISHARANN HERO**
Gloomtide Shipwreck	-	*0*	*Faction Terrain Feature*	

FACTION	ALLIES
Idoneth Deepkin	Cities of Sigmar (**AELF** units only), Daughters of Khaine, Stormcast Eternals, Sylvaneth

KHARADRON OVERLORDS				
WARSCROLL	**UNIT SIZE**	**POINTS**	**BATTLEFIELD ROLE**	**NOTES**
Arkanaut Company	10	100	Battleline	
Arkanaut Frigate	1	250	Behemoth	Single. Battleline in a Barak-Zilfin army
Arkanaut Ironclad	1	490	Behemoth	Single
Aether-Khemist	1	90	Leader	Single
Aetheric Navigator	1	95	Leader	Single
Arkanaut Admiral	1	125	Leader	Single
Bjorgen Thundrik	1	150	Leader	Single, Unique. These units must be taken as a set. Although taken as a set, each is a separate unit.
Thundrik's Profiteers	4			
Brokk Grungsson, Lord-Magnate of Barak-Nar	1	225	Leader	Single, Unique
Endrinmaster with Dirigible Suit	1	190	Leader	Single
Endrinmaster with Endrinharness	1	105	Leader	Single
Endrinriggers	3	120		Battleline if general is an Endrinmaster with Dirigible Suit
Grundstok Gunhauler	1	155		Single. Battleline in a Barak-Urbaz army
Grundstok Thunderers	5	135		Battleline in a Barak-Nar army
Skywardens	3	115		Battleline if general is an Endrinmaster with Dirigible Suit

FACTION	ALLIES
Kharadron Overlords	Cities of Sigmar (**DISPOSSESSED** and **IRONWELD ARSENAL** units only), Fyreslayers, Stormcast Eternals

WARSCROLL	UNIT SIZE	POINTS	BATTLEFIELD ROLE	NOTES
LUMINETH REALM-LORDS				
Vanari Starshard Ballista	1	125	Artillery	Single
Vanari Auralan Wardens	10	145	Battleline	For each Vanari Auralan Wardens unit included in an army, 1 Vanari Auralan Sentinels unit or 1 Vanari Dawnriders unit can be included in the army as a Battleline unit.
Alarith Spirit of the Mountain	1	375	Behemoth	Single
Alarith Stonemage	1	130	Leader	Single
Ellania and Ellathor, Eclipsian Warsages	1	285	Leader	Single, Unique. This unit can be included as an ally in any army that has an **ORDER** general.
Hurakan Windmage	1	120	Leader	Single
The Light of Eltharion	1	250	Leader	Single, Unique
Lyrior Uthralle, Warden of Ymetrica	1	215	Leader	Single, Unique
Myari Lightcaller	1	240	Leader	Single, Unique. These units must be taken as a set. Although taken as a set, each is a separate unit.
Myari's Purifiers	3			
Scinari Calligrave	1	115	Leader	Single
Scinari Cathallar	1	145	Leader	Single
Scinari Loreseeker	1	170	Leader	Single
Sevireth, Lord of the Seventh Wind	1	345	Leader	Single, Unique
Vanari Bannerblade	1	120	Leader	Single
Vanari Lord Regent	1	155	Leader	Single
Archmage Teclis and Celennar, Spirit of Hysh	1	740	Leader, Behemoth	Single, Unique
Avalenor, the Stoneheart King	1	415	Leader, Behemoth	Single, Unique
Alarith Stoneguard	5	120		Battleline in an Ymetrica army
Hurakan Spirit of the Wind	1	265		Single
Hurakan Windchargers	5	155		Battleline in a Helon army
Vanari Auralan Sentinels	10	150		See notes for Vanari Auralan Wardens
Vanari Bladelords	5	130		For each **SCINARI HERO** included in an army, 1 Vanari Bladelords unit can be included in the army as a Battleline unit.
Vanari Dawnriders	5	140		See notes for Vanari Auralan Wardens
Hyshian Twinstones	-	50	*Endless Spell*	
Rune of Petrification	-	75	*Endless Spell*	
Sanctum of Amyntok	-	60	*Endless Spell*	
Shrine Luminor	-	0	*Faction Terrain Feature*	

FACTION	ALLIES
Lumineth Realm-lords	Idoneth Deepkin

10

SERAPHON				
WARSCROLL	**UNIT SIZE**	**POINTS**	**BATTLEFIELD ROLE**	**NOTES**
Engine of the Gods	1	265	Artillery, Leader, Behemoth	Single
Saurus Guard	5	115	Battleline	
Saurus Knights	5	110	Battleline	
Saurus Warriors	10	105	Battleline	
Skinks	10	75	Battleline	
Bastiladon with Ark of Sotek	1	185	Behemoth	Single
Bastiladon with Solar Engine	1	235	Behemoth	Single
Stegadon	1	265	Behemoth	Single. Battleline in a Thunder Lizard army
Kixi-Taka, the Diviner	1		Leader	Single, Unique. These units must be taken as a set. Although taken as a set, each is a separate unit.
Klaq-Trok	1	225		
The Starblood Stalkers	4			
Lord Kroak	1	430	Leader	Single, Unique
Ripperdactyl Chief	1	85	Leader	Single
Saurus Astrolith Bearer	1	150	Leader	Single
Saurus Eternity Warden	1	125	Leader	Single
Saurus Oldblood	1	120	Leader	Single
Saurus Scar-Veteran on Cold One	1	110	Leader	Single
Saurus Sunblood	1	125	Leader	Single
Skink Priest	1	80	Leader	Single
Skink Starpriest	1	130	Leader	Single
Skink Starseer	1	145	Leader	Single
Slann Starmaster	1	265	Leader	Single
Terradon Chief	1	80	Leader	Single
Saurus Oldblood on Carnosaur	1	270	Leader, Behemoth	Single
Saurus Scar-Veteran on Carnosaur	1	215	Leader, Behemoth	Single
Skink Oracle on Troglodon	1	270	Leader, Behemoth	Single
Stegadon with Skink Chief	1	305	Leader, Behemoth	Single
Chameleon Skinks	5	115		
Kroxigor	3	150		
Razordon Hunting Pack	4	95		
Ripperdactyl Riders	3	95		
Salamander Hunting Pack	4	120		
Terradon Riders	3	115		
Realmshaper Engine	-	0	*Faction Terrain Feature*	

FACTION	ALLIES
Seraphon	Cities of Sigmar, Stormcast Eternals

STORMCAST ETERNALS			
WARSCROLL	**UNIT SIZE**	**POINTS**	**BATTLEFIELD ROLE**	**NOTES**
Celestar Ballista	1	120	Artillery	Single
Judicators	5	150	Battleline	
Liberators	5	95	Battleline	
Vindictors	5	140	Battleline	
Astreia Solbright	1	215	Leader	Single, Unique
Aventis Firestrike, Magister of Hammerhal	1	325	Leader	Single, Unique
Averon Stormsire	1	280	Leader	Single, Unique. These units must be taken as a set. Although taken as a set, each is a separate unit.
Stormsire's Cursebreakers	2			
Celestant-Prime, Hammer of Sigmar	1	325	Leader	Single, Unique
Errant-Questor	1	140	Leader	Single
Gavriel Sureheart	1	130	Leader	Single, Unique
Knight-Arcanum	1	150	Leader	Single
Knight-Azyros	1	110	Leader	Single
Knight-Heraldor	1	110	Leader	Single
Knight-Incantor	1	130	Leader	Single
Knight-Questor	1	110	Leader	Single
Knight-Venator	1	120	Leader	Single
Knight-Vexillor	1	120	Leader	Single
Knight-Vexillor with Banner of Apotheosis	1	125	Leader	Single
Knight-Zephyros	1	110	Leader	Single
Lord-Aquilor	1	185	Leader	Single
Lord-Arcanum	1	160	Leader	Single
Lord-Arcanum on Celestial Dracoline	1	225	Leader	Single
Lord-Arcanum on Gryph-charger	1	215	Leader	Single
Lord-Arcanum on Tauralon	1	300	Leader	Single
Lord-Castellant	1	130	Leader	Single
Lord-Celestant	1	110	Leader	Single
Lord-Celestant on Dracoth	1	215	Leader	Single
Lord-Celestant Gardus Steel Soul	1	120	Leader	Single, Unique
Lord-Exorcist	1	95	Leader	Single
Lord-Imperatant	1	160	Leader	Single
Lord-Ordinator	1	150	Leader	Single
Lord-Relictor	1	110	Leader	Single
Lord-Veritant	1	120	Leader	Single
Neave Blacktalon	1	120	Leader	Single, Unique
Vandus Hammerhand	1	280	Leader	Single, Unique
Yndrasta, the Celestial Spear	1	300	Leader	Single, Unique
Drakesworn Templar	1	450	Leader, Behemoth	Single
Lord-Celestant on Stardrake	1	540	Leader, Behemoth	Single
Aetherwings	3	45		
Annihilators	3	190		
Castigators	3	75		
Decimators	5	185		
Dracothian Guard Concussors	2	235		
Dracothian Guard Desolators	2	205		
Dracothian Guard Fulminators	2	235		
Dracothian Guard Tempestors	2	205		
Evocators	5	225		
Evocators on Celestial Dracolines	3	280		
Gryph-hounds	6	130		
Praetors	3	155		

STORMCAST ETERNALS				
WARSCROLL	UNIT SIZE	POINTS	BATTLEFIELD ROLE	NOTES
Prosecutors	3	95		
Protectors	5	185		
Retributors	5	205		
Sequitors	5	130		Battleline if general is a LORD-ARCANUM
Steelheart's Champions	3	110		Single, Unique
The Farstriders	3	110		Single, Unique
Vanguard-Hunters	5	110		Battleline if general is a Lord-Aquilor
Vanguard-Palladors	3	185		
Vanguard-Raptors with Hurricane Crossbows	3	150		
Vanguard-Raptors with Longstrike Crossbows	3	185		
Celestial Vortex	-	*30*	*Endless Spell*	
Dais Arcanum	-	*30*	*Endless Spell*	
Everblaze Comet	-	*110*	*Endless Spell*	

FACTION	ALLIES
Stormcast Eternals	Cities of Sigmar, Idoneth Deepkin, Fyreslayers, Lumineth Realm-lords, Kharadron Overlords, Seraphon, Sylvaneth

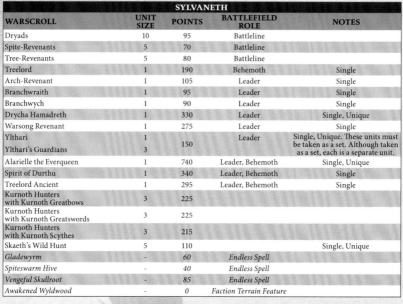

SYLVANETH				
WARSCROLL	**UNIT SIZE**	**POINTS**	**BATTLEFIELD ROLE**	**NOTES**
Dryads	10	95	Battleline	
Spite-Revenants	5	70	Battleline	
Tree-Revenants	5	80	Battleline	
Treelord	1	190	Behemoth	Single
Arch-Revenant	1	105	Leader	Single
Branchwraith	1	95	Leader	Single
Branchwych	1	90	Leader	Single
Drycha Hamadreth	1	330	Leader	Single, Unique
Warsong Revenant	1	275	Leader	Single
Ylthari	1	150	Leader	Single, Unique. These units must be taken as a set. Although taken as a set, each is a separate unit.
Ylthari's Guardians	3			
Alarielle the Everqueen	1	740	Leader, Behemoth	Single, Unique
Spirit of Durthu	1	340	Leader, Behemoth	Single
Treelord Ancient	1	295	Leader, Behemoth	Single
Kurnoth Hunters with Kurnoth Greatbows	3	225		
Kurnoth Hunters with Kurnoth Greatswords	3	225		
Kurnoth Hunters with Kurnoth Scythes	3	215		
Skaeth's Wild Hunt	5	110		Single, Unique
Gladewyrm	-	60	*Endless Spell*	
Spiteswarm Hive	-	40	*Endless Spell*	
Vengeful Skullroot	-	85	*Endless Spell*	
Awakened Wyldwood	-	0	*Faction Terrain Feature*	

FACTION	ALLIES
Sylvaneth	Cities of Sigmar (**DISPOSSESSED** units only and only if general is **IRONBARK**), Fyreslayers (only if general is **IRONBARK**), Idoneth Deepkin, Stormcast Eternals

CHAOS

BEASTS OF CHAOS				
WARSCROLL	**UNIT SIZE**	**POINTS**	**BATTLEFIELD ROLE**	**NOTES**
Gors	10	75	Battleline	
Ungors	10	70	Battleline	
Chaos Gargant	1	180	Behemoth	Single
Chimera	1	220	Behemoth	Single
Cygor	1	140	Behemoth	Single
Ghorgon	1	170	Behemoth	Single
Jabberslythe	1	165	Behemoth	Single
Beastlord	1	95	Leader	Single
Doombull	1	115	Leader	Single
Dragon Ogor Shaggoth	1	185	Leader	Single
Grashrak Fellhoof	1	150	Leader	Single, Unique. These units must be taken as a set. Although taken as a set, each is a separate unit.
Grashrak's Despoilers	5			
Great Bray-Shaman	1	100	Leader	Single
Tzaangor Shaman	1	135	Leader	Single
Bestigors	10	135		Battleline if general is a Beastlord or GREAT BRAY-SHAMAN
Bullgors	3	155		Battleline if general is a Doombull
Centigors	5	90		
Chaos Spawn	1	55		
Chaos Warhounds	10	80		
Cockatrice	1	95		Single
Dragon Ogors	3	150		Battleline if general is a Dragon Ogor Shaggoth
Razorgors	1	55		
Tuskgor Chariots	1	65		
Tzaangor Enlightened	3	95		
Tzaangor Enlightened on Discs of Tzeentch	3	180		
Tzaangor Skyfires	3	195		
Tzaangors	10	175		Battleline if general is a Tzaangor Shaman
Ungor Raiders	10	90		
Doomblast Dirgehorn	-	45	*Endless Spell*	
Ravening Direflock	-	50	*Endless Spell*	
Wildfire Taurus	-	110	*Endless Spell*	
Herdstone	-	0	*Faction Terrain Feature*	

FACTION	ALLIES
Beasts of Chaos	Slaves to Darkness

BLADES OF KHORNE

WARSCROLL	UNIT SIZE	POINTS	BATTLEFIELD ROLE	NOTES
Skull Cannons	1	140	Artillery	
Flesh Hounds	5	105	Battleline	
Bloodletters	10	115	Battleline	
Bloodreavers	10	80	Battleline	
Blood Warriors	10	210	Battleline	
Aspiring Deathbringer	1	85	Leader	Single
Bloodmaster, Herald of Khorne	1	90	Leader	Single
Bloodsecrator	1	125	Leader	Single
Bloodstoker	1	85	Leader	Single
Exalted Deathbringer	1	85	Leader	Single
Herald of Khorne on Blood Throne	1	125	Leader	Single
Korghos Khul	1	165	Leader	Single, Unique
Lord of Khorne on Juggernaut	1	155	Leader	Single
Mighty Lord of Khorne	1	135	Leader	Single
Scyla Anfingrimm	1	110	Leader	Single, Unique
Skarr Bloodwrath	1	105	Leader	Single, Unique
Skullgrinder	1	90	Leader	Single
Skullmaster, Herald of Khorne	1	125	Leader	Single
Skulltaker	1	130	Leader	Single
Slaughterpriest	1	110	Leader	Single
Valkia the Bloody	1	140	Leader	Single, Unique
Bloodthirster of Insensate Rage	1	280	Leader, Behemoth	Single
Bloodthirster of Unfettered Fury	1	295	Leader, Behemoth	Single
Skarbrand	1	380	Leader, Behemoth	Single, Unique
Wrath of Khorne Bloodthirster	1	310	Leader, Behemoth	Single
Bloodcrushers	3	130		Battleline if general is a Skullmaster, Herald of Khorne
Garrek's Reavers	5	65		Single, Unique
Karanak	1	150		Single, Unique
Khorgoraths	1	110		
Mighty Skullcrushers	3	170		Battleline if general is a Lord of Khorne on Juggernaut
Riptooth	1			Single, Unique. These units must be taken as a set. Although taken as a set, each is a separate unit.
Magore's Fiends	3	125		
Skullreapers	5	205		
Wrathmongers	5	155		
Bleeding Icon	-	50	*Invocation*	
Hexgorger Skulls	-	60	*Invocation*	
Wrath-Axe	-	85	*Invocation*	
Skull Altar	-	0	*Faction Terrain Feature*	

FACTION	ALLIES
Blades of Khorne	Maggotkin of Nurgle, Slaves to Darkness (excluding units that can or must be given a Mark of Chaos)

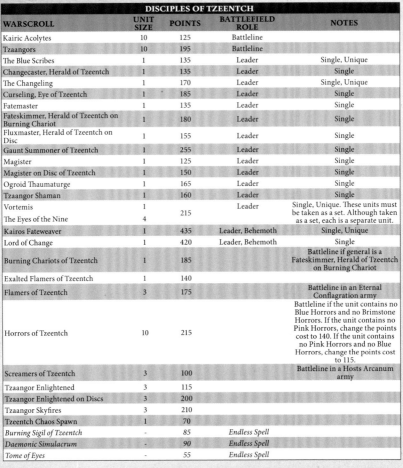

DISCIPLES OF TZEENTCH

WARSCROLL	UNIT SIZE	POINTS	BATTLEFIELD ROLE	NOTES
Kairic Acolytes	10	125	Battleline	
Tzaangors	10	195	Battleline	
The Blue Scribes	1	135	Leader	Single, Unique
Changecaster, Herald of Tzeentch	1	135	Leader	Single
The Changeling	1	170	Leader	Single, Unique
Curseling, Eye of Tzeentch	1	185	Leader	Single
Fatemaster	1	135	Leader	Single
Fateskimmer, Herald of Tzeentch on Burning Chariot	1	180	Leader	Single
Fluxmaster, Herald of Tzeentch on Disc	1	155	Leader	Single
Gaunt Summoner of Tzeentch	1	255	Leader	Single
Magister	1	125	Leader	Single
Magister on Disc of Tzeentch	1	150	Leader	Single
Ogroid Thaumaturge	1	165	Leader	Single
Tzaangor Shaman	1	160	Leader	Single
Vortemis	1	215	Leader	Single, Unique. These units must be taken as a set. Although taken as a set, each is a separate unit.
The Eyes of the Nine	4			
Kairos Fateweaver	1	435	Leader, Behemoth	Single, Unique
Lord of Change	1	420	Leader, Behemoth	Single
Burning Chariots of Tzeentch	1	185		Battleline if general is a Fateskimmer, Herald of Tzeentch on Burning Chariot
Exalted Flamers of Tzeentch	1	140		
Flamers of Tzeentch	3	175		Battleline in an Eternal Conflagration army
Horrors of Tzeentch	10	215		Battleline if the unit contains no Blue Horrors and no Brimstone Horrors. If the unit contains no Pink Horrors, change the points cost to 140. If the unit contains no Pink Horrors and no Blue Horrors, change the points cost to 115.
Screamers of Tzeentch	3	100		Battleline in a Hosts Arcanum army
Tzaangor Enlightened	3	115		
Tzaangor Enlightened on Discs	3	200		
Tzaangor Skyfires	3	210		
Tzeentch Chaos Spawn	1	70		
Burning Sigil of Tzeentch	-	85	*Endless Spell*	
Daemonic Simulacrum	-	90	*Endless Spell*	
Tome of Eyes	-	55	*Endless Spell*	

FACTION	ALLIES
Disciples of Tzeentch	Hedonites of Slaanesh, Slaves to Darkness (excluding units that can or must be given a Mark of Chaos)

HEDONITES OF SLAANESH				
WARSCROLL	UNIT SIZE	POINTS	BATTLEFIELD ROLE	NOTES
Blissbarb Archers	11	180	Battleline	
Daemonettes	10	140	Battleline	
Hellstriders with Claw-spears	5	135	Battleline	
Hellstriders with Hellscourges	5	135	Battleline	
Bladebringer, Herald on Exalted Chariot	1	265	Leader	Single
Bladebringer, Herald on Hellflayer	1	215	Leader	Single
Bladebringer, Herald on Seeker Chariot	1	190	Leader	Single
The Contorted Epitome	1	255	Leader	Single
Dexcessa, the Talon of Slaanesh	1	280	Leader	Single, Unique
Infernal Enrapturess, Herald of Slaanesh	1	140	Leader	Single
Lord of Pain	1	155	Leader	Single
The Masque	1	135	Leader	Single, Unique
Shardspeaker of Slaanesh	1	150	Leader	Single
Sigvald, Prince of Slaanesh	1	265	Leader	Single, Unique
Synessa, the Voice of Slaanesh	1	260	Leader	Single, Unique
Viceleader, Herald of Slaanesh	1	140	Leader	Single
Glutos Orscollion, Lord of Gluttony	1	475	Leader, Behemoth	Single, Unique
Keeper of Secrets	1	420	Leader, Behemoth	Single
Shalaxi Helbane	1	405	Leader, Behemoth	Single, Unique
Syll'Esske, the Vengeful Allegiance	1	210	Leader, Behemoth	Single, Unique
Blissbarb Seekers	5	220		
Exalted Chariot	1	200		Single
Fiends	3	200		
Hellflayer	1	155		Single
Myrmidesh Painbringers	5	160		Battleline if general is a Lord of Pain
Seeker Chariots	1	130		Battleline in a Godseekers army
Seekers	5	140		
Slaangor Fiendbloods	3	150		
Slickblade Seekers	5	230		
Symbaresh Twinsouls	5	185		Battleline if general is a Lord of Pain
The Dread Pageant	4	130		Single, Unique
Dreadful Visage	-	90	*Endless Spell*	
Mesmerising Mirror	-	80	*Endless Spell*	
Wheels of Excruciation	-	100	*Endless Spell*	
Fane of Slaanesh	-	0	*Faction Terrain Feature*	

FACTION	ALLIES
Hedonites of Slaanesh	Disciples of Tzeentch, Maggotkin of Nurgle, Slaves to Darkness (excluding units that can or must be given a Mark of Chaos)

WARSCROLL	UNIT SIZE	POINTS	BATTLEFIELD ROLE	NOTES
MAGGOTKIN OF NURGLE				
Plaguebearers	10	110	Battleline	
Putrid Blightkings	5	165	Battleline	
Epidemius, Tallyman of Nurgle	1	180	Leader	Single, Unique
Fecula Flyblown	1	190	Leader	Single, Unique. These units must be taken as a set. Although taken as a set, each is a separate unit.
The Wurmspat	2			
Festus the Leechlord	1	140	Leader	Single, Unique
Gutrot Spume	1	145	Leader	Single, Unique
Harbinger of Decay	1	145	Leader	Single
Horticulous Slimux	1	225	Leader	Single, Unique
Lord of Afflictions	1	180	Leader	Single
Lord of Blights	1	135	Leader	Single
Lord of Plagues	1	135	Leader	Single
Poxbringer, Herald of Nurgle	1	135	Leader	Single
Rotbringer Sorcerer	1	120	Leader	Single
Sloppity Bilepiper, Herald of Nurgle	1	130	Leader	Single
Spoilpox Scrivener, Herald of Nurgle	1	125	Leader	Single
Bloab Rotspawned	1	230	Leader, Behemoth	Single, Unique
The Glottkin	1	395	Leader, Behemoth	Single, Unique
Great Unclean One	1	350	Leader, Behemoth	Single
Morbidex Twiceborn	1	235	Leader, Behemoth	Single, Unique
Orghotts Daemonspew	1	220	Leader, Behemoth	Single, Unique
Rotigus	1	345	Leader, Behemoth	Single, Unique
Beasts of Nurgle	1	125		
Nurglings	3	90		
Plague Drones	3	195		
Pusgoyle Blightlords	2	185		Battleline if general is a Lord of Afflictions
Feculent Gnarlmaw	-	0	*Faction Terrain Feature*	

FACTION	ALLIES
Maggotkin of Nurgle	Blades of Khorne, Hedonites of Slaanesh, Slaves to Darkness (excluding units that can or must be given a Mark of Chaos)

WARSCROLL	UNIT SIZE	POINTS	BATTLEFIELD ROLE	NOTES
			SKAVEN	
Plagueclaw	1	160	Artillery	Single
Warp Lightning Cannon	1	185	Artillery	Single
Warplock Jezzails	3	145	Artillery	
Clanrats	20	130	Battleline	
Stormvermin	10	110	Battleline	
Doomwheel	1	165	Behemoth	Single
Hell Pit Abomination	1	240	Behemoth	Single
Arch-Warlock	1	175	Leader	Single
Clawlord	1	105	Leader	Single
Deathmaster	1	115	Leader	Single
Grey Seer	1	140	Leader	Single
Master Moulder	1	95	Leader	Single
Plague Priest	1	85	Leader	Single
Skritch Spiteclaw	1	120	Leader	Single, Unique. These units must be taken as a set. Although taken as a set, each is a separate unit.
Spiteclaw's Swarm	4			
Warlock Bombardier	1	125	Leader	Single
Warlock Engineer	1	125	Leader	Single
Grey Seer on Screaming Bell	1	265	Leader, Behemoth	Single
Lord Skreech Verminking	1	330	Leader, Behemoth	Single, Unique
Plague Priest on Plague Furnace	1	245	Leader, Behemoth	Single
Thanquol on Boneripper	1	405	Leader, Behemoth	Single, Unique
Verminlord Corruptor	1	285	Leader, Behemoth	Single
Verminlord Deceiver	1	345	Leader, Behemoth	Single
Verminlord Warbringer	1	305	Leader, Behemoth	Single
Verminlord Warpseer	1	335	Leader, Behemoth	Single
Doom-Flayer	1	60		Single
Giant Rats	6	40		Battleline if general is **MASTERCLAN** or **CLANS MOULDER** and all other units are **CLANS MOULDER**
Gutter Runners	5	65		Battleline if general is **MASTERCLAN** or **CLANS ESHIN** and all other units are **CLANS ESHIN**
Night Runners	10	85		Battleline if general is **MASTERCLAN** or **CLANS ESHIN** and all other units are **CLANS ESHIN**
Packmasters	3	60		
Plague Censer Bearers	5	65		Battleline if general is **MASTERCLAN** or **CLANS PESTILENS** and all other units are **CLANS PESTILENS**
Plague Monks	10	85		Battleline if general is **MASTERCLAN** or **CLANS PESTILENS** and all other units are **CLANS PESTILENS**
Rat Ogors	2	95		Battleline if general is **MASTERCLAN** or **CLANS MOULDER** and all other units are **CLANS MOULDER**
Rat Swarms	2	60		
Ratling Gun	1	65		Single
Skryre Acolytes	5	65		Battleline if general is **MASTERCLAN** or **CLANS SKRYRE** and all other units are **CLANS SKRYRE**
Stormfiends	3	315		Battleline if general is **MASTERCLAN** or **CLANS SKRYRE** and all other units are **CLANS SKRYRE**
Warpfire Thrower	1	70		Single
Warp-Grinder	1	75		Single

SKAVEN				
WARSCROLL	**UNIT SIZE**	**POINTS**	**BATTLEFIELD ROLE**	**NOTES**
Bell of Doom	-	85	Endless Spell	
Vermintide	-	80	Endless Spell	
Warp Lightning Vortex	-	90	Endless Spell	
Gnawhole	-	0	Faction Terrain Feature	

FACTION	**ALLIES**
Skaven	Maggotkin of Nurgle (only if general is **CLANS PESTILENS**)

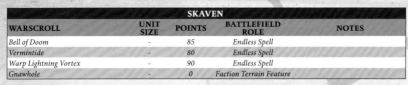

SLAVES TO DARKNESS

WARSCROLL	UNIT SIZE	POINTS	BATTLEFIELD ROLE	NOTES
Chaos Chariots	1	105	Battleline	
Chaos Knights	5	170	Battleline	
Chaos Marauders	10	90	Battleline	
Chaos Marauder Horsemen	5	110	Battleline	
Chaos Warriors	10	200	Battleline	
Chaos Warshrine	1	185	Behemoth	Single
Mutalith Vortex Beast	1	175	Behemoth	Single
Slaughterbrute	1	165	Behemoth	Single
Soulgrinder	1	235	Behemoth	Single
Chaos Lord	1	120	Leader	Single
Chaos Lord on Daemonic Mount	1	155	Leader	Single
Chaos Lord on Karkadrak	1	225	Leader	Single
Chaos Lord on Manticore	1	255	Leader	Single
Chaos Sorcerer Lord	1	115	Leader	Single
Chaos Sorcerer Lord on Manticore	1	270	Leader	Single
Daemon Prince	1	210	Leader	Single
Darkoath Chieftain	1	85	Leader	Single
Darkoath Warqueen	1	90	Leader	Single
Exalted Hero of Chaos	1	90	Leader	Single
Gaunt Summoner on Disc of Tzeentch	1	230	Leader	Single
Ogroid Myrmidon	1	135	Leader	Single
Theddra Skull-Scryer	1	150	Leader	Single, Unique. These units must be taken as a set. Although taken as a set, each is a separate unit.
Godsworn Hunt	5			
Archaon the Everchosen	1	830	Leader, Behemoth	Single, Unique
Be'lakor, the Dark Master	1	360	Leader, Behemoth	Single, Unique
Chosen	5	145		
Corvus Cabal	9	70		Battleline in an Idolators army
Cypher Lords	8	70		Battleline in an Idolators army
Chaos Spawn	1	55		
Fomoroid Crusher	1	110		Single
Furies	6	95		
Gorebeast Chariots	1	130		
Iron Golems	8	75		Battleline in an Idolators army
Khagra's Ravagers	4	125		Single, Unique. These units must be taken as a set. Although taken as a set, each is a separate unit.
Mindstealer Sphiranx	1	95		Single
Raptoryx	6	85		
Scions of the Flame	8	75		Battleline in an Idolators army
Spire Tyrants	9	70		Battleline in an Idolators army
Splintered Fang	10	75		Battleline in an Idolators army
The Unmade	9	75		Battleline in an Idolators army
Untamed Beasts	9	70		Battleline in an Idolators army
Varanguard	3	280		Battleline in a Host of the Everchosen army
Eightfold Doom-Sigil	-	*50*	*Endless Spell*	
Darkfire Daemonrift	-	*100*	*Endless Spell*	
Realmscourge Rupture	-	*85*	*Endless Spell*	

FACTION	ALLIES
Slaves to Darkness	Beasts of Chaos, Blades of Khorne, Disciples of Tzeentch, Maggotkin of Nurgle, Hedonites of Slaanesh

DEATH

FLESH-EATER COURTS				
WARSCROLL	**UNIT SIZE**	**POINTS**	**BATTLEFIELD ROLE**	**NOTES**
Crypt Ghouls	10	95	Battleline	
Royal Terrorgheist	1	305	Behemoth	Single. Battleline in a Gristlegore army
Royal Zombie Dragon	1	295	Behemoth	Single. Battleline in a Gristlegore army
Abhorrant Archregent	1	245	Leader	Single
Abhorrant Ghoul King	1	165	Leader	Single
Crypt Ghast Courtier	1	70	Leader	Single
Crypt Haunter Courtier	1	115	Leader	Single
Crypt Infernal Courtier	1	130	Leader	Single
Duke Crakmarrow	1	135	Leader	Single, Unique. These units must be taken as a set. Although taken as a set, each is a separate unit.
The Grymwatch	6			
Varghulf Courtier	1	160	Leader	Single
Abhorrant Ghoul King on Royal Terrorgheist	1	445	Leader, Behemoth	Single
Abhorrant Ghoul King on Royal Zombie Dragon	1	445	Leader, Behemoth	Single
Crypt Flayers	3	180		Battleline in a Blisterskin army or if general is a Crypt Infernal Courtier
Crypt Horrors	3	125		Battleline in a Hollowmourne army or if general is a Crypt Haunter Courtier
Cadaverous Barricade	-	55	*Endless Spell*	
Chalice of Ushoran	-	70	*Endless Spell*	
Corpsemare Stampede	-	110	*Endless Spell*	
Charnel Throne	-	0	*Faction Terrain Feature*	

FACTION	ALLIES
Flesh-eater Courts	Soulblight Gravelords

NIGHTHAUNT				
WARSCROLL	UNIT SIZE	POINTS	BATTLEFIELD ROLE	NOTES
Chainrasp Horde	10	95	Battleline	
Grimghast Reapers	10	155	Battleline	
Hexwraiths	5	150	Battleline	
Spirit Hosts	3	125	Battleline	
Black Coach	1	220	Behemoth	Single
The Briar Queen	1	175	Leader	Single, Unique. These units must be taken as a set. Although taken as a set, each is a separate unit.
Thorns of the Briar Queen	6			
Cairn Wraith	1	70	Leader	Single
Dreadblade Harrow	1	100	Leader	Single
Guardian of Souls with Nightmare Lantern	1	135	Leader	Single
Knight of Shrouds	1	100	Leader	Single
Knight of Shrouds on Ethereal Steed	1	120	Leader	Single
Krulghast Cruciator	1	120	Leader	Single
Kurdoss Valentian, the Craven King	1	180	Leader	Single, Unique
Lady Olynder, Mortarch of Grief	1	215	Leader	Single, Unique
Lord Executioner	1	90	Leader	Single
Reikenor the Grimhailer	1	165	Leader	Single, Unique
Spirit Torment	1	115	Leader	Single
Tomb Banshee	1	80	Leader	Single
Bladegheist Revenants	10	190		
Chainghasts	2	75		
Dreadscythe Harridans	10	160		
Glaivewraith Stalkers	4	65		
Myrmourn Banshees	4	75		
Mortalis Terminexus	-	85	*Endless Spell*	
Shyish Reaper	-	70	*Endless Spell*	
Vault of Souls	-	85	*Endless Spell*	

FACTION	ALLIES
Nighthaunt	Soulblight Gravelords

25

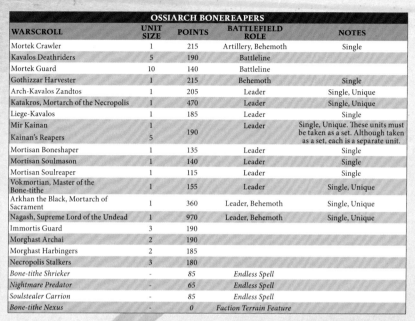

OSSIARCH BONEREAPERS				
WARSCROLL	**UNIT SIZE**	**POINTS**	**BATTLEFIELD ROLE**	**NOTES**
Mortek Crawler	1	215	Artillery, Behemoth	Single
Kavalos Deathriders	5	190	Battleline	
Mortek Guard	10	140	Battleline	
Gothizzar Harvester	1	215	Behemoth	Single
Arch-Kavalos Zandtos	1	205	Leader	Single, Unique
Katakros, Mortarch of the Necropolis	1	470	Leader	Single, Unique
Liege-Kavalos	1	185	Leader	Single
Mir Kainan	1	190	Leader	Single, Unique. These units must be taken as a set. Although taken as a set, each is a separate unit.
Kainan's Reapers	5			
Mortisan Boneshaper	1	135	Leader	Single
Mortisan Soulmason	1	140	Leader	Single
Mortisan Soulreaper	1	115	Leader	Single
Vokmortian, Master of the Bone-tithe	1	155	Leader	Single, Unique
Arkhan the Black, Mortarch of Sacrament	1	360	Leader, Behemoth	Single, Unique
Nagash, Supreme Lord of the Undead	1	970	Leader, Behemoth	Single, Unique
Immortis Guard	3	190		
Morghast Archai	2	190		
Morghast Harbingers	2	185		
Necropolis Stalkers	3	180		
Bone-tithe Shrieker	-	85	*Endless Spell*	
Nightmare Predator	-	65	*Endless Spell*	
Soulstealer Carrion	-	85	*Endless Spell*	
Bone-tithe Nexus	-	0	*Faction Terrain Feature*	

FACTION	ALLIES
Ossiarch Bonereapers	None

SOULBLIGHT GRAVELORDS				
WARSCROLL	UNIT SIZE	POINTS	BATTLEFIELD ROLE	NOTES
Deadwalker Zombies	20	115	Battleline	
Deathrattle Skeletons	10	85	Battleline	
Dire Wolves	10	135	Battleline	
Mortis Engine	1	200	Behemoth	Single
Terrorgheist	1	305	Behemoth	Battleline in an Avengorii Dynasty army
Zombie Dragon	1	295	Behemoth	Battleline in an Avengorii Dynasty army
Gorslav the Gravekeeper	1		Leader	
Torgillius the Chamberlain	1		Leader	
Watch Captain Halgrim	1	605	Leader	Single, Unique. These units must be taken as a set. Although taken as a set, each is a separate unit.
Kosargi Nightguard	2			
Vargskyr	1			
Vyrkos Blood-born	3			
Belladamma Volga, First of the Vyrkos	1	200	Leader	Single, Unique
Prince Duvalle	1	200	Leader	Single, Unique. These units must be taken as a set. Although taken as a set, each is a separate unit.
The Crimson Court	3			
Kritza, the Rat Prince	1	95	Leader	Single, Unique
Lady Annika, the Thirsting Blade	1	110	Leader	Single, Unique
Lauka Vai, Mother of Nightmares	1	285	Leader	Single, Unique
Necromancer	1	125	Leader	Single
Radukar the Beast	1	315	Leader	Single, Unique. Cannot be included in the same army as Radukar the Wolf.
Radukar the Wolf	1	150	Leader	Single, Unique. Cannot be included in the same army as Radukar the Beast.
Vampire Lord	1	140	Leader	Single
Vengorian Lord	1	280	Leader	Single
Wight King	1	115	Leader	Single
Wight King on Skeletal Steed	1	130	Leader	Single
Bloodseeker Palanquin	1	290	Leader, Behemoth	Single
Coven Throne	1	310	Leader, Behemoth	Single
Mannfred von Carstein, Mortarch of Night	1	380	Leader, Behemoth	Single, Unique
Nagash, Supreme Lord of the Undead	1	970	Leader, Behemoth	Single, Unique
Neferata, Mortarch of Blood	1	365	Leader, Behemoth	Single, Unique
Prince Vhordrai	1	455	Leader, Behemoth	Single, Unique
Vampire Lord on Zombie Dragon	1	435	Leader, Behemoth	Single
Black Knights	5	120		Battleline in a Legion of Blood army
Blood Knights	5	195		Battleline in a Kastelai Dynasty army
Corpse Cart with Balefire Brazier	1	80		Single
Corpse Cart with Unholy Lodestone	1	80		Single
Fell Bats	3	75		
Grave Guard	10	140		Battleline if general is a **WIGHT KING**
The Sepulchral Guard	7	80		Single, Unique
Vargheists	3	155		Battleline in a Legion of Night army

FACTION	ALLIES
Soulblight Gravelords	Flesh-eater Courts, Nighthaunt

PITCHED BATTLE PROFILES

DESTRUCTION

GLOOMSPITE GITZ				
WARSCROLL	**UNIT SIZE**	**POINTS**	**BATTLEFIELD ROLE**	**NOTES**
Shootas	20	140	Battleline	
Stabbas	20	150	Battleline	
Aleguzzler Gargant	1	165	Behemoth	Single
Arachnarok Spider with Flinger	1	230	Behemoth	Single
Arachnarok Spider with Spiderfang Warparty	1	225	Behemoth	Single
Mangler Squigs	1	275	Behemoth	Single
Skitterstrand Arachnarok	1	200	Behemoth	Single
Dankhold Troggboss	1	250	Leader	Single
Fungoid Cave-Shaman	1	95	Leader	Single
Loonboss	1	75	Leader	Single
Loonboss on Giant Cave Squig	1	110	Leader	Single
Loonboss with Giant Cave Squig	1	105	Leader	Single
Madcap Shaman	1	80	Leader	Single
Mollog	1	175	Leader	Single, Unique
Scuttleboss on Gigantic Spider	1	105	Leader	Single
Skragrott, the Loonking	1	230	Leader	Single, Unique
Webspinner Shaman	1	85	Leader	Single
Zarbag	1	185	Leader	Single, Unique. These units must be taken as a set. Although taken as a set, each is a separate unit.
Zarbag's Gitz	8			
Loonboss on Mangler Squigs	1	310	Leader, Behemoth	Single
Webspinner Shaman on Arachnarok Spider	1	295	Leader, Behemoth	Single
Boggleye	1			
Brewgit	1			
Scaremonger	1	190		Single. These units must be taken as a set. Although taken as a set, each is a separate unit.
Shroomancer	1			
Spiker	1			
Boingrot Bounderz	5	105		
Dankhold Troggoth	1	190		
Fellwater Troggoths	3	155		Battleline if general is a Dankhold Troggboss
Loonsmasha Fanatics	5	145		
Rippa's Snarlfangs	3	70		Single, Unique
Rockgut Troggoths	3	145		Battleline if general is a Dankhold Troggboss
Sneaky Snufflers	6	75		
Spider Riders	5	100		Battleline if general is **SPIDERFANG**
Sporesplatta Fanatics	5	135		
Squig Herd	12	160		Battleline if general is **MOONCLAN**
Squig Hoppers	10	180		Battleline if general is a Loonboss on Giant Cave Squig or Loonboss on Mangler Squigs
Malevolent Moon	-	80	*Endless Spell*	
Mork's Mighty Mushroom	-	100	*Endless Spell*	
Scrapskuttle's Arachnacauldron	-	50	*Endless Spell*	
Scuttletide	-	85	*Endless Spell*	
Bad Moon Loonshrine	-	0	*Faction Terrain Feature*	

FACTION	ALLIES
Gloomspite Gitz	Orruk Warclans

PITCHED BATTLE PROFILES

OGOR MAWTRIBES				
WARSCROLL	**UNIT SIZE**	**POINTS**	**BATTLEFIELD ROLE**	**NOTES**
Gnoblar Scraplauncher	1	130	Artillery	Single
Ironblaster	1	130	Artillery	Single
Ogor Gluttons	6	260	Battleline	
Stonehorn Beastriders	1	320	Behemoth	Single. Battleline if general is **BEASTCLAW RAIDERS**
Thundertusk Beastriders	1	285	Behemoth	Single. Battleline if general is **BEASTCLAW RAIDERS**
Butcher	1	135	Leader	Single
Firebelly	1	125	Leader	Single
Hrothgorn	1	170	Leader	Single, Unique. These units must be taken as a set. Although taken as a set, each is a separate unit.
Hrothgorn's Mantrappers	3			
Icebrow Hunter	1	125	Leader	Single
Slaughtermaster	1	140	Leader	Single
Tyrant	1	160	Leader	Single
Frostlord on Stonehorn	1	430	Leader, Behemoth	Single
Frostlord on Thundertusk	1	385	Leader, Behemoth	Single
Huskard on Stonehorn	1	340	Leader, Behemoth	Single
Huskard on Thundertusk	1	335	Leader, Behemoth	Single
Frost Sabres	2	55		Battleline if general is an **ICEBROW HUNTER**
Gnoblars	20	120		
Gorgers	1	80		
Icefall Yhetees	3	120		Battleline if general is a **THUNDERTUSK**
Ironguts	4	245		Battleline if general is **GUTBUSTERS**
Leadbelchers	4	180		Battleline if general is **GUTBUSTERS**
Maneaters	3	180		
Mournfang Pack	2	160		Battleline if general is **BEASTCLAW RAIDERS**
Great Mawpot	-	*0*	*Faction Terrain Feature*	

FACTION	ALLIES
Ogor Mawtribes	Gloomspite Gitz (Aleguzzler Gargant units and **TROGGOTH** units only)

ORRUK WARCLANS

WARSCROLL	UNIT SIZE	POINTS	BATTLEFIELD ROLE	NOTES
Gutrippaz	10	180	Battleline	
Savage Orruks	10	130	Battleline	
Hedkrakka, Gob of Gork	1	235	Leader	Single, Unique. These units must be taken as a set. Although taken as a set, each is a separate unit.
Hedkrakka's Madmob	3			
Killaboss on Great Gnashtoof	1	200	Leader	Single
Killaboss with Stab-grot	1	140	Leader	Single
Maniak Weirdnob	1	130	Leader	Single
Murknob with Belcha-banna	1	115	Leader	Single
Orruk Megaboss	1	160	Leader	Single
Orruk Warchanter	1	120	Leader	Single
Orruk Weirdnob Shaman	1	120	Leader	Single
Savage Big Boss	1	110	Leader	Single
Swampcalla Shaman with Pot-grot	1	125	Leader	Single
Wardokk	1	85	Leader	Single
Wurrgog Prophet	1	170	Leader	Single
Gordrakk, the Fist of Gork	1	580	Leader, Behemoth	Single, Unique
Kragnos, the End of Empires	1	695	Leader, Behemoth	Single, Unique
Megaboss on Maw-krusha	1	495	Leader, Behemoth	Single
Hobgrot Slittaz	10	95		
Ironskull's Boyz	4	85		Single, Unique
Man-skewer Boltboyz	3	120		
Morgok's Krushas	3	95		Single, Unique
Orruk Ardboys	5	95		Battleline in an Ironjawz or Big Waaagh! army
Orruk Brutes	5	150		Battleline in an Ironjawz or Big Waaagh! army
Orruk Gore-gruntas	3	170		Battleline in an Ironjawz or Big Waaagh! army
Savage Big Stabbas	2	110		
Savage Boarboy Maniaks	5	150		Battleline in a Bonesplitterz army
Savage Boarboys	5	140		Battleline in a Bonesplitterz or Big Waaagh! army
Savage Orruk Arrowboys	10	130		Battleline in a Bonesplitterz or Big Waaagh! army
Savage Orruk Morboys	10	130		Battleline in a Bonesplitterz army

FACTION	ALLIES
Orruk Warclans	Gloomspite Gitz

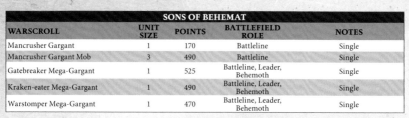

SONS OF BEHEMAT				
WARSCROLL	UNIT SIZE	POINTS	BATTLEFIELD ROLE	NOTES
Mancrusher Gargant	1	170	Battleline	Single
Mancrusher Gargant Mob	3	490	Battleline	Single
Gatebreaker Mega-Gargant	1	525	Battleline, Leader, Behemoth	Single
Kraken-eater Mega-Gargant	1	490	Battleline, Leader, Behemoth	Single
Warstomper Mega-Gargant	1	470	Battleline, Leader, Behemoth	Single

FACTION	ALLIES
Sons of Behemat	None

ADDITIONAL PITCHED BATTLE PROFILES

ENDLESS SPELLS				
WARSCROLL	**UNIT SIZE**	**POINTS**	**BATTLEFIELD ROLE**	**NOTES**
Aethervoid Pendulum	-	65	Endless Spell	
Burning Head	-	20	Endless Spell	
Chronomantic Cogs	-	45	Endless Spell	
Emerald Lifeswarm	-	60	Endless Spell	
Geminids of Uhl-Gysh	-	80	Endless Spell	
Horrorghast	-	65	Endless Spell	
Lauchon the Soulseeker	-	55	Endless Spell	
Malevolent Maelstrom	-	65	Endless Spell	
Prismatic Palisade	-	40	Endless Spell	
Purple Sun of Shyish	-	70	Endless Spell	
Quicksilver Swords	-	90	Endless Spell	
Ravenak's Gnashing Jaws	-	55	Endless Spell	
Shards of Valagharr	-	70	Endless Spell	
Soulscream Bridge	-	70	Endless Spell	
Soulsnare Shackles	-	65	Endless Spell	
Suffocating Gravetide	-	50	Endless Spell	
Umbral Spellportal	-	70	Endless Spell